Stand Up And Fight!

A Handbook On Spiritual Warfare

Bill and Pam Malone

© Copyright Bill and Pam Malone

All rights reserved. No part of this publication may be reproduced, stored in a retrieval system, or transmitted in any form or by any means—electronic, mechanical, photo-copying, recording, or otherwise—without the prior permission of the publisher and copyright owner. The only exception is brief quotations in printed reviews.

Unless indicated otherwise, Scripture quotations are taken from the HOLY BIBLE, NEW INTERNATIONAL VERSION. Copyright 1973, 1978, 1984 International Bible Society. Used by permission of Zondervan Bible Publishers.

The views expressed in this book are the authors' and do not necessarily reflect those of the publisher.

Published/printed in the United States of America.

7710-T Cherry Park Dr, Ste 224
Houston, TX 77095
www.WorldwidePublishingGroup.com
(713) 766-4271

Paperback: 978-1-387-05370-4
Hardcover: 978-1-387-05372-8

Contents

Dedication	iv
Introduction	vii
Our Power and Authority	- 1 -
Satan Attacks	- 5 -
Stressed Out	- 9 -
Fear or Faith	- 15 -
Be Bold	- 19 -
Spiritual Discipline	- 25 -
The Warrior Mentality	- 29 -
Satan Hits Us Below the Belt	- 35 -
The Physical and Spiritual Battle	- 41 -
How to Combat a Furious Adversary	- 45 -
The Importance of Unity	- 51 -
The Battle Belongs to The Lord	- 57 -
We Are Our Own Worst Enemy!	- 61 -
The Spirit Man	- 67 -
God's Army	- 71 -
The Bride	- 77 -
Praying for Our Nation	- 83 -
A Gift of The Spirit	- 87 -
Victory in Jesus	- 93 -
The Authors	- 99 -

Other Books by Bill and Pam Malone

Come To The Waters
http://bit.ly/Come-To-The-Waters

Hear the incredible account of how prayer, unity, and perseverance helped to change the spiritual climate of the San Francisco Bay Area. Your prayer life will be inspired as you see examples of God's miraculous power in everyday living. Throughout this book you will read of God's provision and the call to bring Pray U.S.A.! into being. Over 55 pictures are included to help you visualize what took place. Allow this book to open your heart to pray more, listen with new ears, and step out with fresh boldness"

How To Make Prayer Exciting
http://bit.ly/Make-Prayer-Exciting

Prayer on boats, motorcycles, and in airplanes? What kind of prayer lifestyle is this? An exciting one! Join Bill and Pam on their journey to discover new ways to pray with their family, their community, and their church. This book will ignite your prayer life. You will find yourself praying wherever you go, whatever you do, or whomever you're with!

Healing Prayer

"Bill and Pam share a sound, comprehensive view of many aspects of healing prayer in this great book. I particularly appreciated its practicality and simple prayers for beginners. This would make a perfect curriculum for Sunday School classes and small group studies."
Doris M. Wagner, Minister

31 Days of Healing

This is a daily guide for spiritual growth and healing. The Word of God is alive and is the power that releases the healing anointing of Christ Jesus into your life. The Bible says, "Have faith in God. Faith comes from hearing and hearing by the Word of God". Our faith is a "doing faith". Whatever your infirmity is, take a step of faith into that healing and you will sense faith rising within you.

DEDICATION

Crystal, Delynne, Brielle, and Jonathan

Delynne, Jonathan, Brielle and Crystal Collett... we dedicate this book to you. You each have unique personalities and God-given gifts. Use those gifts to strengthen, encourage and to bring out the best in those around you. We pray that this book will be a blessing and a help to you as you navigate this life.

With all our love,
GB and GP

INTRODUCTION

Life is full of ups and downs. We wrote this book to try and help its readers to be able to avoid and deal more effectively with the downs that come our way. As we have tried to analyze our own lives we have seen that many of the low points were caused by our own bad decisions. Our Father, God, desires the best for His children and that is why He gave His best, His only Son, Jesus the Christ.

Our decisions should always come after we have taken time to pray, asking God for His input, then proceed as He has indicated. The obvious is for us to take the time with our Father and then be able to discern His voice from our will and Satan's input. Jesus never did anything except what His Father was telling Him to do. We must learn and practice this practical teaching in our lives daily. As we do, we will be able to differentiate God's voice from the other voices just mentioned, our own and Satan's.

This book comes from what we have experienced and observed as we have lived and ministered in this life. You will find real problems, their effects, how they were dealt with and outcomes.

This truly is a handbook on spiritual warfare and how to be overcomers against the evil supernatural that comes only to kill, steal and destroy God's people.

We cannot emphasize enough how much better your life will be when you take the time to ask God for His input into your life. When you pray for wisdom and direction, always have a pen and paper to write down whatever comes to your mind. Please, don't try to analyze it, just write down what comes to your mind. When you begin your prayer, command in the name of Jesus for your own thoughts and will to be silenced and for any evil supernatural input to be silenced. You can always ask God afterwards for confirmation or directions regarding what you have written down. He doesn't mind you putting out a "fleece" to verify what you feel He has said.

May the Lord bless you and give you wisdom and insight as you read this book and put into practice principles found in it. You are overcomers and victorious already because Father, God, loves you so much.

Victory in Jesus.

Bill and Pam

Our Power and Authority

Why do so many people today believe that the spiritual gifts and miracles seen in the Bible stopped when the last Apostle died? There is absolutely nothing in the Bible that would promote a belief such as this. Satan is the liar. He is the one who promotes that belief so the Christians who accept and believe this way of thinking will not be able to hinder his rule in their lives and the lives of all whom they touch. Satan comes to only kill, steal and destroy. He has stolen the power and authority from those who believe his lies.

When did Jesus ever pray to His Father, asking Him (Father, God) to heal someone, to cast out a demon or to calm the water? Only on one occasion did Jesus speak to His Father before performing a miracle. That was just before Jesus spoke to Lazarus to come forth from the grave. John 11:41-43 (NKJV) *"...Father, I thank You that You have heard Me. And I know that You always hear Me, but because of the people who are standing by, I said this, that they may believe that You sent Me...Lazarus come forth."* He was giving His Father thanks for the miracle about to happen.

We must certainly pray. Jesus taught His disciples to pray. One of the most powerful prayers is by Jesus in John 17 when He prayed for Himself and His believers. We must realize that prayer is two-way communication with our Father. We ask and then listen for His response and obey His directive to us. It is through this dialog that we develop a closer relationship and learn to recognize our Father's voice. When we recognize His voice then we can reject the tempting voice from Satan and our own voice which may be negative and untrue and contradict the will of our Father.

Jesus tells us in John 10:10 (AMP), *"The sheep that are My own hear and listen to My voice; and I know them and they follow Me."* Jesus only did what the Father was doing. They had a very close relationship. When Jesus healed the cripple at the well, there were many other infirm people there. But, Jesus healed just one. For whatever reason, that is the only one that Father wanted healed at that time. Jesus knew His Father's will and did not try to heal the others.

There are times to pray and there are times to speak in the authority that we have been given. Our authority comes from Jesus Christ and our indwelling Holy Spirit. John 17:18 (AMP), *"Just as You sent Me into the world, I also have sent them into the world."* The "them" that Jesus talks about is us. John 14:12 (KJV), *"Verily, verily, I say unto you, He that believeth on Me, the works that I do shall he do also; and greater works than these shall he do;*

because I go to My Father." We must first believe in Jesus. Then whenever you see "verily, verily" or "truly, truly," what comes after will stir doubt and unbelief in our mind. The doubt and unbelief is, "Well, that was Jesus, I certainly can't do what He did." We won't when these doubts and unbelief come into us. Jesus has never lied, nor could He. There is no need for Him to say, "verily, verily" or "truly, truly," except to emphasize to us that we *will* be able to do what He says. Doubt and unbelief are the tools of Satan to keep us from our God given authority.

When Jesus says, *"greater works than these shall he do,"* He means that as Christians worldwide begin using their authority, more miracles will take place. When Jesus was here on earth, He could only be in one place at a time. Now wherever Christians are walking in their power and authority, there is Jesus. So, greater works are being done. The reason that Jesus has given us this power is found in John 14:13 (NIV), *"And I will do whatever you ask in my name, so the Father may be glorified in the Son."* If we do not walk in our authority, no glory can be given to God. All Jesus has ever wanted to do was bring glory to Father, God. This should be our goal as well, doing all that we can to bring healing and deliverance to the lost and hurting of this world so that God will get the glory. This will plunder Satan's kingdom and populate Heaven.

No longer will we be silenced. No longer will we succumb to the lies of the enemy saying that we have no spiritual power. We will stand on the truth, the Word of God as to who we are. We will pray more, listen more, and do the will of our Father. We will stand up and fight with the power given to us from Above.

SATAN ATTACKS

Satan dealt my husband, Bill and me, Pam Malone a low blow after the 2004 National Day of Prayer (NDP). We believed that this was the best NDP that we had ever experienced. Not because of anything we had done personally, but because of the interest, the number of events, a worldwide prayer meeting, etc. that took place on that day. Exactly one week after the NDP and three months after we opened the Healing Rooms of Tampa Bay in Tampa, FL, I was hospitalized for five days. I went seven days and seven nights without sleep so you can imagine the shape I was in—physically, mentally, emotionally and spiritually. I basically "flipped out". You would think I would just have "passed out", but that wasn't the case. I was admitted to the psychiatric ward and assigned a psychiatrist who diagnosed me at that time as bi-polar/manic depressive. Looking back, it could have been so much worse, but this was bad enough. While I was in the hospital, Bill "resigned" us from all volunteer activities and made my health, well-being and our personal relationship the #1 priority.

    We spent four months going to doctors, taking different medications, doing different health food remedies and, of course, praying. It was a very difficult time for both of us to say the least. The next week, I had an appointment with another sleep specialist (doctor #7). Each doctor did what they knew to do and prescribed the medication or health food remedy they thought would help. Each thing made slight improvements, but still no natural sleep. We both felt that we were in a desperate situation and knew the power of prayer as we have both experienced healing miracles. We know what the Word of God says in Psalms 4:8 (AMP), *"In peace I will both lie down and sleep."* Isaiah 29:10 (AMP), *"For the Lord has poured out on you the spirit of deep sleep."* Psalms 127:2, *"For he gives blessings to his beloved in sleep."* And Proverbs 3:24 (AMP), *"When you lie down, you shall not be afraid; yes, you shall lie down, and your sleep shall be sweet."*

Sometimes when you're under such severe attack, you need to ask others to help you by standing in the gap and praying and doing spiritual warfare for you. This is what we did. We had everyone we knew or had the opportunity to share our dilemma with, to pray. I took advantage of receiving prayer at every church or prayer group we attended. I felt like the widow woman in the Bible who just kept going back until the healing took place.

Discouragement, frustration, depression, anger, doubt and unbelief - you name it, we experienced all of it. Then there were times we stood in complete strong faith, knowing that God was healing me. I was going to bed at night after doing all the soothing, calming things I knew to do; hot baths complete with lavender oil, candlelight, drinking sleepy time tea with honey, massage, sleep music - everything we knew to make the atmosphere more conducive to rest and sleep. Six hours later, still no natural sleep. Out came the sleeping pills again. There were many nights I would just lie there all night and never fall asleep. I was determined not to take the sleeping pills my body was so addicted to. However, when morning came I was so wiped out, I would take them so I could get a few hours' sleep to somewhat function. You would think that with little or no sleep at night that surely, I would be able to lie down sometime during the day for a little nap, but not so.

I was telling a friend of mine about my recent saga. I relayed to her that my health situation was in an "emergency state." This was after a night of maybe two hours of medicated sleep. I was sharing how this whole "circus" was almost funny if you didn't have to live it out! The previous week, I had been to a doctor who had given me a medication that was to try to "even me out" so I could sleep at night. One of the side effects of this was possible weight gain. Sure enough, I gained 13 pounds after being on this medication only four weeks. And still no sleep. This was especially discouraging to me, as I had lost quite a bit of weight by trying to consume less and eat more healthy foods.

If I could only get some sleep, it would be worth it and then later I could drop the weight. The doctor said there was another medication he knew of where one of the side effects was sleep. He had prescribed it to another patient who also had problems sleeping at night and it seemed to help him. But there were side effects. One was there would be a possibility that my skin could "roll off!" When he said this, I responded, "Excuse me, did I hear you correctly? Please repeat what you just said." I did hear him correctly, my mind wasn't hallucinating, but I replied, "I don't think so." What went through my mind was lying in bed, sleeping, with my skin rolling off onto the sheets. This didn't seem like the right thing to do! We knew that this was an attack of the enemy on my physical and mental health. It had to be battled in the natural realm due to the physical ailments, but more importantly in the spiritual dimension with prayer.

STRESSED OUT

We found ourselves becoming so stressed due to the not knowing and inability of the doctors to find and cure Pam. But, we knew that God knew what we were going through. We don't live in a perfect world but, God has provided His strength for us to be victorious over our situations. We must learn to rely on Him at these times in our lives.

Have you ever found yourself stressed out during a time that you really want to experience peace and thanksgiving? What about during the Thanksgiving holidays and the Christmas season? It seems like no matter how hard we try, we seem to somehow get caught up in stress. We want to change and rather than look to our self (which causes stress), look and reach up to God and rest in Him. He is the only one who can give us the true peace that we are seeking.

When people are tugging at you and you seem to be pulled in so many different directions and then a family crisis comes along on top of it all, it's very easy to fall into the stressed-out mode. If you're anything like us (human), somehow, we start fussing with each other rather than realizing that the enemy has come in to cause our division. We must step back a moment, take a deep breath and realize that we are on the same team. Now stop and begin to pray for God's wisdom, unity and strength to overcome the evil supernatural attack that we are under. Also, ask for the Father's keener discernment so that we can recognize Satan's tactics before we fall into his entrapment.

One morning before our quiet time before the Lord, we started to get grumpy with each other. But, praise the Lord, we recognized the schemes of the enemy to try and keep us from our time with the Father and said, "Oh, no you don't. This is the day the Lord has made – let us rejoice and be glad in it." We know God's plan is for good and not evil.

As we went into our quiet time, we prayed and asked Father to speak to us. Our pads and pens were ready to start writing. The Lord spoke to Pam, saying, "You are on My path. Look upward to Me, not sideways to each other. I will help you, I will show you, I will provide for you. Look all around your home and see the results of you and Bill working together just as I have ordained for you to do. You make beautiful music together, each doing your part – seeking guidance and direction from Me. Don't lash out at each other. This hurts Me and it hurts you. Don't continue to wound your spirits within. You are a beautiful creation together, you fit together perfectly. As husband and wife, as ministry partners and all else I call you to do. Ask Me for more patience, love for each other, compassion and whatever you are lacking. Remember, I'm here to give you everything you need to complete My calling. Do not attack each other. This is what the enemy wants you to do so that nothing productive will get done for Me. You must be wise to the schemes of the enemy and stop wasting time and falling into his traps. This is not a one-time thing, a one day thing, this is a moment by moment battle. Be wise – come to Me. I am wisdom and I give wisdom to those who ask. Remember, you are writing the book, "Stand Up and Fight" and I want My people to learn from your experiences. I want each one of you to experience a victorious life, now. You are in the Army of God and you will have joy in all situations, trials and circumstances. My joy is your strength. I am training My people for these times in which I have chosen you to live. Be aware and be discerning. There is no time to waste."

We both prayed, "Lord, help us to see more clearly and to be aware of the times in which we are living. Help us to remember we are in a continuous battle. May we always keep our eyes focused on You. Please forgive us for falling for one of Satan's schemes again. We know he is the father of lies and all he tries to do is divide anyway he can. Pick us up, Lord, unite us and fill us more with Your spirit. We want less of ourselves and more of You. We love You and we have decided to follow Jesus - no matter what! We pray all of this in the mighty name of Jesus. Amen."

We feel that the Lord is reminding us that we are not fighting each other. Whether it is husband/wife, parents/children or any other combination, the point is that the fight is not against flesh and blood, but against the principalities in dark places. The battle will manifest in the natural or physical realm, but we are to battle with the spiritual power that Father, God has given to us. Just as Paul reminds us in Ephesians 6:10-18 (NKJV),

> *"Finally, my brethren, be strong in the Lord and in the power of His might. Put on the whole armor of God, that you may be able to stand against the wiles of the devil. For we do not wrestle against flesh and blood, but against principalities, against powers, against spiritual hosts of wickedness in the heavenly places. Therefore, take up the whole armor of God that you may be able to withstand in the evil day, and having done all, to stand. Stand therefore having girded your waist with truth, having put on the breastplate of righteousness and having shod your feet with the preparation of the gospel of peace; above all, taking the shield of faith with which you will be able to quench all the fiery darts of the wicked one. And take the helmet of salvation, and the sword of the spirit, which is the word of God; praying always with all prayer and supplication in the spirit, being watchful to this end with all perseverance and supplication for all the saints."*

So, we must always remember what is really going on. We know it's very clear in God's word, but sometimes, in the heat of battle we forget and attack each other.

There are many times in the Bible when battles are going on, confusion comes and everybody gets mixed up. They start attacking their own team members, rather than the enemy. We do this to each other sometimes because we just forget what God's truth is. We know better, but we just mess up. When we repent, God is quick to forgive and will help all involved to have peace. "God, grant us, Your people, the wisdom and discernment to know what's going on at all times and not allow Satan to get us side tracked and into a battle that keeps us from doing Your will. Help us to learn quickly and not continue to fall for the same divisiveness over and over. Thank You, Lord, that you have given us the spiritual ammunition to fight the good fight and then to rest in You. We are so grateful that we serve You, the living God, Creator of all things that are, that were and that ever will be to come. In Jesus' name, we pray. Amen."

FEAR OR FAITH

We each have a choice on how we will live our lives. We can either live in fear, which is directly from Satan and void of the love of God which casts out all fear, or by faith. When we choose to live by faith, we know we please God because that is the basis of His whole gospel message. Hebrews 11:6 (NKJV) tells us, *"But without faith it is impossible to please Him, for he who comes to God must believe that He is, and that He is a rewarder of those who diligently seek Him."* In other words, we believe God before we see the result. By this faith, Abraham left his home not knowing where he was going. Noah built a large boat in an area where there was no water. They didn't see the result. They acted on faith only. Many did not see God's promise come to pass in their lifetime or benefit directly from their action of faith. Many were and are being mocked, beaten, beheaded, crucified, but by faith remained true to the faith and examples to mankind.

The part these people played was in preparing the way for those that followed. They did not receive their reward here, but made it possible for others to receive the gift of salvation. They were called to plow the ground. We each have our calling and by faith we will complete that calling. It could be plowing the ground, planting the seed or reaping the harvest.

All of us like our comfort zone. Few people realize that the true comfort zone is found only in Jesus Christ and in doing what He has placed us here to complete. He is our Rock and Fortress. He is the only one we can truly trust as we put our faith in Him, listen to Him and obey His direction in our lives.

Bill and I (Pam) had to leave a church due to a difference in the way the pastor felt we were handling an area wide, non-denominational prayer meeting. It hurt us greatly that our church and pastor were unable to go along with the unity effort that we were putting forth. Our parting was like the apostle Paul and Barnabas. We agreed that we each had different callings to fulfill for the Lord. It's not that one was right and the other wrong, just different paths to follow. Believe me, we sought the Lord's direction before bringing together, evangelicals, Pentecostals, charismatics, non-denominations, all who loved the Lord, but worshipped in different fashions. The Body of Christ is made up of different personalities (congregations) and that is a good thing. God doesn't read the sign in front of the place where we worship. He reads our individual hearts.

In multiple prayer times and laying out fleeces we felt a certainty that God was calling us to help unify His Body. When we expressed this idea of a unified prayer meeting we were met with many who could not go along with this idea. It did discourage us, but we had faith that we had heard from God and had to continue.

A couple of years later, after having monthly all church prayer meetings, hosting pastors' prayer meetings and luncheons, God called us to do a prayer meeting on a boat in San Francisco Bay. He said not to worry about the cost, He wanted His Body to go out on the bay and pray for this area. Again, there was skepticism, but once again by faith we rented a yacht for a four-hour cruise on the bay. On the day of the prayer cruise there were over three hundred people on board from many different countries. Over twenty pastors took turns praying and many different worship groups led us all in worshipping our Lord. We were to have paid the owner before the cruise, but we told him we did not have the money yet as we would be taking up a collection during the cruise. He graciously allowed us to continue.

The pastor who was to take up the offering asked us how much was needed and we told him $7,000.00. He said, "What! I need to go pray". When the collection was taken, the entire amount needed was there. Those who counted the offering said that there was no large offering; all small amounts and the coins and bills were all even amounts. The next day's newspaper announced that the drug gangs in Oakland had joined together so that they could have better control and more sales, but on the day of the prayer cruise there was the largest drug bust in Oakland's history that took place and shut down these gangs. The gangs understood the power in unity.

Those on the prayer cruise and many other pastors we talked to afterward who were not on board, agreed that it was due to the unity of the Body of Christ praying together that broke the evil supernatural powers and exposed the drug gangs. By faith we stepped out to charter a yacht, bring the pastors and Body of Christ together, and the Lord did the rest.

BE BOLD

Bill and I needed a time to get away and relax. He loves the water and taking cruises so we booked a cruise to the Caribbean. We booked with Carnival Cruise Lines, not realizing that they are known for the younger, partying crowd. Halloween happened to be that week and there were advertisements for Halloween parties to be held all over the ship and with cobwebs hanging from all the ceilings. We learned a long time ago that Halloween is Satan's high and holy night and we wanted no part of it!

We talked together about organizing a Christian event on that night and asked God for His direction. We felt an anointing to go forward with our idea, but didn't know where to start. So, we went to the purser's desk in the lobby of the ship and spoke with them about our request of having a Christian event on the night of Halloween since we don't participate in that event. A lady next to us said that she wanted to attend, but the purser interjected that we needed authority from the hotel director. The lady then asked if we would pray for her friend and we said, "Sure, after we finish here."

When we finished with the purser, we went to where that lady and her friend were, in one of the small lounges off the lobby. The lady told us her request and we prayed. After the prayer, the lady who asked us to pray for her friend said that she had felt heat on her arm while we were praying and that her carpel tunnel syndrome was healed. She said her husband was miraculously healed from pornography and saved by God and he had been carrying a cross across the United States to proclaim Jesus and they would be there for him to give his conversion experience.

We found out that the hotel director oversees everything on the ship except what the captain does in getting the ship from port to port. The purser told us that she would talk to the hotel director and get back to us.

That afternoon she called and said we had an appointment with the director the next morning. When we went to his office, he invited us in and his first words were, "I am all for what you are planning. But, first, would you pray for me?" What a surprise and a great beginning. The Lord laid out the path and all we had to do was walk down it.

We told the director that we would like to have a facility where we could have worship songs, a short Gospel message and testimonies from those that came. He said we could use the library or the main lounge. We had seen the library and that was rather small so we chose the main lounge. He then called in his audio/visual man and told him to get us whatever we needed. Wow! What favor. God really pulled this one off. But, He wasn't finished.

The a/v man asked for a program for the night and he would have everything ready at the appropriate time. The hotel director also called the purser and told her that we would be coming down and to get our information to put an announcement into the daily shipboard newspaper announcing this event.

On Halloween, there was a great article regarding the evening service for those who would like to attend. They also had a disclaimer that it was not a Carnival Cruise event. We arrived at the lounge and met the a/v man and gave him a CD of Christian worship songs and directions as to the timing of each of the specific songs we desired to be played that night. We had no idea if anyone would show up. So, we waited.

Soon people started coming in. As we began our worship, there were about fifty to sixty people who had come in. After our worship and message, we started to pray for different areas as we felt led. We had asked the Hotel Director for a list of workers so that we could pray for them. He gave us a full list of the staff's names and countries where they were from. So, now, we not only prayed by name for each of them, but also for their country.

We opened it up to people who would like to share. One never knows what will take place with an open mic. But people came forward and gave awesome testimonies of God working in their lives. Finally, the husband of the lady who was healed of the carpel tunnel syndrome came forward. He said that he was an alcoholic and addicted to pornography. One day he was in XXX rated movie and the Lord spoke to him to leave, this was not for him. He was confused and didn't know what was happening to him so he got out of there. When he was outside a conviction of shame came over him, yet a feeling of love that he had never known or felt before.

He felt such peace and release that he wanted to tell someone. He saw a hitchhiker, picked him up and started telling him about being in a porn movie and what had happened. The hitchhiker became fearful and said, "Let me out of this car". After that the man who had been delivered and set free from his addictions said that he was going to spend the rest of his life giving his testimony regarding the Love of Jesus. So, he literally built a large cross and carried it as he walked north to south and east to west all across America and into Europe preaching the Gospel. What a testimony on Halloween night on a Carnival Cruise ship. God had this set up just waiting for us to be bold enough to request a night of worship.

As we were leaving, there was a maid that was there to clean up the lounge. She came to us and said she was confused about Buddha, Jesus, Mormonism and the other religions. She was from the Philippines and growing up and on board the ship with so many different ethnic peoples and religions, she was confused as to what was the truth. She asked if she could talk to us after she was off duty. We said, "sure, what time?" She said, "1:00 AM." Oh, me. Of course, with an opportunity that the Lord supplies, our obedience is required.

We went back to our cabin and rested until the time to meet with the maid. We met in the lounge and sat down and began to learn of the stories that she had been told and of her background. We always want to hear from the person about where they stand on religion and their beliefs. Then we can start from that point to teach them the Gospel. As we talked with her about the truth that she was seeking, her countenance and appearance started to brighten noticeably. We asked if she would like to receive Jesus as her Lord and Savior and she said, "Yes". We led her in prayer right in the main lounge of that party ship and she received Jesus. She was totally changed when we parted.

SPIRITUAL DISCIPLINE

Our spiritual discipline is so important in fighting our spiritual battles. Don't take this area lightly. Our armed forces are trained to utilize discipline daily for their own safety and to defeat the enemy. We are in God's army and must understand that to defeat our spiritual enemy, we must be spiritually disciplined as well.

We tend to know more about our physical discipline because we can see, feel and touch our bodies. We need to discipline our flesh because it is at war with our spirit. Our flesh cries out give me more, but we generally restrain ourselves because we know more is not better: more french fries, more ice cream, and on and on. It takes discipline to eat correctly and give your body what it needs to function at its best. It takes effort to do this, to fight against what your desires are calling for. It takes discipline to eat what your body needs and not give in to your own cravings. If we do give in to our fleshly desires, our body will become weakened and subject to disease and not able to function as God desires.

Most of our spiritual warfare comes in the form of our physical pain and suffering. The pain and suffering in our bodies may come from our own mistreatment of God's Temple. He is the one who created us and placed us in this shell we call our body and gave us rule and reign over the Temple where He dwells. We are the caretakers and unfortunately, much of the time we do not take very good care of what has been given to us. If we are not giving this Temple the proper nourishment, rest and exercise, then we will be more susceptible to natural disaster and to the schemes of the enemy.

Give Satan an inch and he will take a mile. The realm of the evil supernatural is to find ways of blocking the Christian from fulfilling the reason God placed him here on earth. We all have a job, a calling of God, to complete while we are here.

Physical disabilities, where we must spend our time, energy and finances on ourselves, are a prime way to get us off track and keep us from our God given work. We play right into Satan's hands when we do not care for our bodies. Satan can still inflict physical problems, with God's permission as he did with Job, even if we are taking excellent care of ourselves. We must stop aiding the enemy by abusing our bodies.

Now is the time to stand up and fight and say, "I will no longer abuse this Temple of God. I will feed, exercise and care for this body because it is God's property, He loves me so much and has given me everything so that I might have victory here and now. I will no longer aide the enemy who is trying to keep me from my fullest potential in serving my God".

Our spiritual body needs to be fed properly to stay healthy and accomplish God's will in our lives. The foods that are required for our spirit man are prayer, reading and studying the Word, memorizing the Scriptures, taking communion regularly, praising the Lord and giving thanks in all circumstances. One of the most important spiritual disciplines, and yet the least used, is taking time to listen to God. One of the ways to get started is to set aside a time with pen and paper in a quiet place. Pray and ask God what He wants to say to you. Write down whatever comes to mind. If you don't feel you've heard anything, try again the next day.

God's promise to us is that we will hear His voice. John 10:27(NKJV), *"My sheep hear my voice, and I know them, and they follow me."* When Pam first started this, it took ten days before she felt the Lord speak to her. He will test you to see if you're serious. Jesus said that He never did anything except what the Father was telling Him. Then He said that "as the Father has sent Me, I am sending you (each one of us)". Remember that the Spirit that was in Jesus is the same Spirit that is in us today. We can hear from God! Just give Him a chance.

Galatians 5:16 (NIV), *"So I say, live by the Spirit, and you will not gratify the desires of the sinful nature."* It is so important to feed the spiritual nature in us so that we will be spiritually strong to overcome the desires of the flesh. Remember that it is the spiritual man that never dies. The body will decay, but it is very important to take care of it properly now. Proper diet, exercise and sleep are ways we can help our physical bodies stay in shape. Our physical bodies are the vessels that house our spiritual man. We will be much better prepared for our spiritual battles when our physical bodies and our spiritual man are working at peak performance.

The Warrior Mentality

To "fight the good fight and win the race" we must have a warrior mentality. This has meant many different things to Bill and me over the years in the battles in which we have been engaged.

Many times, I (Pam) felt I couldn't go on, things were just too difficult. In these times of despair, I had to reach out to others to help guide me in the truth. I needed their strength, their prayers and their perspective. There are several people close to me who have always been there for me. Of course, Bill, my faithful husband was always by my side. He would pray for me when I couldn't pray, he would read the Bible to me when I couldn't read or comprehend. We both knew that the Word of God was powerful and would not return void, but would accomplish the plan God had for it to do. So, we always knew my spirit was being nurtured, encouraged, strengthened and made more whole.

My brother, Bob, who is a Christian businessman, was always there for me when I needed him. Sometimes he would just listen, and then sometimes he would ask questions to make me think about what I was saying or feeling. Bob told me once, when he answered the phone, he could always tell by my tone of voice if I had a good or bad night as this would vastly affect my thinking, outlook and attitude. At the time, the only sleep I could get at all was with medication. Sometimes even that didn't work, so I would have to take more and stay in bed the next day.

Ricky, our son, was there when I needed to talk to him. He is a very loving and compassionate person by nature and has a pastoral anointing over his life. He sometimes had to tell me, "No, Mom, that thinking is not right. That is not what Jesus would say or do".

Many times, during this "battle with insomnia," Bill had to correct my thinking and he would say, "No, Pam that is not the truth. That is not what the Bible says."

Can you see how the lack of sleep can affect everything about you? I consider myself a relatively nice person, at least most of the time. Of course, I was very aware of my shortcomings.

Anger set in as this illness progressed. I would get mad, "God, why won't you just let me sleep so I can live a normal life?" Sometimes I was so weak and "out of it," I didn't want to live. I was tired of fighting. Life didn't seem worth it. Praise the Lord when these horrible times came, the Lord provided me with His needed comfort.

Our mind is Satan's playground. When we become weakened in other areas of our life, such as my lack of sleep in this example, Satan invades our mind to plant untrue and misleading thoughts. He knows that the Word of God says that we are to have the mind of Christ,

Philippians 2:5 (AMP). However, in our weakness Satan will mount an all-out effort to take over our minds. Therefore, it is so important to have a person or people that you can trust and will be there for you to help and guide you in the truths, such as the church family, a pastor, family and friends. If you do not have this back up help, please take steps to find a church, get to know the pastor better and cultivate friendships with others.

Satan is so bold. He knows that every day belongs to the Lord. But, he has been so bold as to try and steal a day and make it fun for the children. It is now one of America's most popular holidays, known as Halloween. The early settlers in America did not celebrate this "holiday" as they were Christians and would not allow any pagan events in the colonies. As time went on and more immigrants came to America, especially in the mid 1800's when many Irish immigrants came here due to the potato famine, they started celebrating this holiday. And it has grown to what it is today.

It is still a pagan holiday, and as we learned of the roots of this celebration, we determined that we would not be a part of it. Satan uses this as his most holy day and Satanists worldwide have special celebrations and sacrifices on this day.

The Lord tells us to avoid every kind of evil, Thessalonians 5:22 and that *"My people are destroyed from lack of knowledge,"* Hosea 4:6 (NIV). We decided that Satan had gone too far in trying to steal one of the days that the Lord had made. As we prayed for wisdom and direction as to what should be done, we felt the Lord said that this is the perfect night to evangelize. What other night do you have many people coming to your door? Why just give them candy that causes cavities? Why not give them something of eternal value?

Since people portray this night as dark and evil, we decided that since we always put up white lights in the front of our house at Christmas, why not put them up early and turn on all the lights in our house to make our property as bright and lit up and inviting as possible. After all, aren't we Christians to be the light of the world? We are going to use this night to glorify God!

So, in 1996 we had had enough of Satan and his deceit of this day. We put white lights all over our bushes and doorway. We had ordered small Bibles with Scripture messages and a salvation prayer. We went to a Christian book store and bought pencils, erasers and small items with Jesus loves you on them. We bought glazed doughnuts, set tables out in the front yard and had hot cider and hot chocolate.

We were ready for the trick or treating to begin. By giving a doughnut and hot drink, each person would have to stop to eat and drink, not just grab and run to the next house. As they were eating and drinking we asked if we could pray a blessing and protection on them for this night. We gave each of them a small Bible and let them choose one of the other gifts that we had for them.

Now when the children get home and empty out their bags of goodies, they will be once again reminded of Jesus by our little gift and their "unusual visit" to our home. We plant seeds of the Gospel and prayer while they are at our house, and then when they get home another little seed of our gifts is now planted in their home. As we plant the seeds, God will water and nurture them into growth.

The first year that we did this in San Francisco, it was extremely successful beyond our wildest dreams or imagination. We must have had close to 200 visitors! Even some of the parents asked if they could have one of the little Bibles. There was a group of teenage boys coming down the street in "high gear." Pam stepped onto the sidewalk and asked them if they would like some doughnuts and hot chocolate? They said, "Sure, why not?" After we chatted a few minutes, as they were ready to leave, we asked them if we could pray for them. You should have seen the shock in their eyes, but they accepted. And we sent them off with a "God bless you," and one hollered back over his shoulder, "And God bless you, too!"

Satan Hits Us Below the Belt

Bill and I arrived home late one evening and were listening to our phone messages from the day. We had several regular ones and then we got "the one" you always dread to receive. It was from our oldest son, Rick. He said to call him as soon as we got in; he had an emergency in his family. We called immediately and learned that Delynne, our oldest granddaughter, who was 14 at the time, had passed out at her basketball game. She had been filming the game and suddenly lost consciousness and fell over. She was immediately helped by the EMT's on the ambulance that was right outside for the game.

Delynne was transported to a rural hospital nearby. A CAT scan revealed a large mass on her brain stem. This facility could do nothing for her and her parents were told that she would have to be transported by helicopter to a major hospital in Lubbock, TX - which was 150 miles away. That night there was very poor visibility and so much wind that the hospital's helicopter was grounded and could not fly. Fortunately, there was a retired Air Force helicopter pilot on duty. He and his crew decided to take the risk to pick up Delynne. One of the crew members was familiar with the area and she assured the pilot she could provide valuable information about the terrain if an emergency landing was necessary.

They were able to make the trip and pick up Delynne. During this whole process, Delynne remained unconscious. Her heart had shut down to 15% capacity and while being incubated, she aspirated into her lungs. Her lungs ability to process her body's vital need for oxygen had now been compromised. The crew frantically worked to keep her alive during the entire return trip. When they arrived back at the hospital in Lubbock, the neurologist was waiting to perform an emergency procedure to relieve the building pressure on her brain. The doctor felt that there was very little that could be done to save Delynne due to the mass on her brain stem and her lungs inability to function properly.

When Delynne's parents, Rick and Minnie Collett, arrived, they were told the bad news. They told the doctors that they must do everything possible to save her. Delynne was stabilized, but still in a coma. The doctors confirmed that the mass on her brain stem was a tumor. The tumor was the size of a lemon and had smashed her brain stem to such an extent that virtually no spinal fluid could reach her brain. The tumor then hemorrhaged causing pressure in her brain. The team of doctors determined they would not be able to keep her alive during the emergency tumor resection surgery – the only option was to wait and see if her heart would strengthen enough for the surgery.

Prayers went out everywhere possible. Five days later, Delynne, still in a coma, was strong enough for the surgery. The surgeon said that it would be a five- to six-hour operation. Delynne was taken to the operating room and about two hours later the surgeon came out and his first words were, "Your prayers have been answered." The tumor just fell out and all he had to do was suction out some of the tentacles. Shouts of joy went up and praise reports were sent back to all who had been praying.

This ordeal left Delynne unable to walk or talk clearly. This happened when she was 14. She is now 24 and still improving. She does daily exercises and is very strong. She holds on to the fence around her backyard and can walk the circumference holding on to the fence unaided. She can also walk with someone holding on to her and she awaits the day she doesn't need her wheelchair. God continues to heal her daily.

When she was four and five years old, she and her family lived with us while our house was being remodeled by her dad. Some mornings she would come up to our bedroom and tell us that the Lord had given her a song, would we like to hear it? This happened on many occasions. She was a very spiritual little girl. Later when she was 8-10 years old, she would accompany us on our ministry trips. After we spoke, Delynne would join us in praying for people. Many times, the Lord would give her prophetic words for the person she was praying for. She had amazing spiritual gifts.

We felt that Satan was trying to take Delynne out through this cancer, but, the Lord hadn't finished with her yet. In all that Delynne has been through, she has maintained such a sweet and loving personality. She ministers to everyone she meets by allowing the love of Jesus to flow through her to all around her. Delynne is standing up and fighting the good fight.

Satan comes to kill, steal and destroy (John 10:10). Somehow, he seems to know the potential in people when they are born and wants them shut down before they can do any damage to his kingdom. Rev. 12:1-4 (NIV) says, *"A great sign appeared in heaven: a woman clothed with the sun, with the moon under her feet and a crown of twelve stars on her head. She was pregnant and cried out in pain as she was about to give birth. Then another sign appeared in heaven: an enormous red dragon with seven heads and ten horns and seven crowns on its heads. Its tail swept a third of the stars out of the sky and flung them to earth. The dragon stood in front of the woman who was about to give birth, so that it might devour her child the moment he was born."* Satan didn't succeed in stopping the Savior of mankind. He didn't stop Delynne, but, he keeps trying. Rev. 12:11 (NIV) states, *"They triumphed over him (Satan) by the blood of the Lamb and by the word of their testimony..."* There were many miracles in Delynne's ordeal and she has a powerful testimony to overcome the evil supernatural deceivers. Thankfully she still retains the spiritual gifts from God that Satan tried to stop.

The Physical and Spiritual Battle

In May of 2015 Pam and I (Bill) traveled to Matador, TX to see two of our grandchildren graduate; Brielle Collett from high school and Crystal from middle school.

We landed in Lubbock, rented a car and made the hour and a half drive to Matador.

The next day, Saturday morning, I (Bill) awoke with excruciating pain in my right lower back. I had a kidney stone years ago and that's exactly what it felt like. I could hardly move due to the pain. Rick and Minnie, our son and daughter-in-law, had just received a call from her Dad and they were on their way over to his house to take him to the hospital. Rick Moyer was at Rick and Minnie's house and had been working with our son, so he said that he would drive us to Lubbock and take us to the hospital.

We arrived at the emergency room mid-morning and had to wait until late afternoon to see a doctor. That was a miserable wait, although the pain subsided some during the wait. When I was taken in, the first thing they did was take a CAT scan of my kidney.

After a while, the doctor came in and told us that I had a mass on my bladder. We had told him previously that we were just visiting for our grandchildren's graduation and that we were from Florida. He said that I had to see a urologist as soon as I returned. I had the feeling that he wanted to admit me due to what he had seen. But, he gave me the CAT scan disc and a prescription for pain medication.

We made it through the visit and graduations thanks to the pain meds. I had already scheduled an appointment with a urologist for the Wednesday after our return. On Monday after our arrival at home, I took the report and disc to the urologist's office so that he would have the information for my appointment on Wednesday.

At the appointment, he did an examination and found a large tumor in my bladder, partially blocking the tube from my kidney and that blockage is what was causing the pain. He took a sample of the tumor and sent it to a lab to see if it was benign or cancerous. We had an appointment for the results on the next Wednesday morning. When he came into the room, he was very somber and said that the result of the biopsy was positive. *It was cancer.* He scheduled surgery for the next morning.

The surgery went well. He said that the tumor was into the muscle and he went into the muscle as far as reasonably possible to extract as much of the cancer as possible. He said that I would need chemotherapy, but probably not radiation. We scheduled an appointment with the oncologist and at that appointment he said radiation was necessary as it aided the chemo in killing the cancer.

So, six weeks of radiation daily, except weekends, and chemo once weekly for between four and five hours on intravenous chemicals of different kinds. When we heard that I had cancer, we sent out prayer requests to all our prayer partners. During this six week period, I was only nauseated one time and felt that my body tolerated this treatment very well. I did as much as I could in preparing my body before and during this treatment with vitamins and healthy eating. I stopped all sugar, soft drinks, red meat and anything with white flower. I juiced carrots and drank five pounds of carrot juice a day. I could buy 25 pounds of organic carrots at Publix grocery store. I did lose strength and appetite, but was still able to go to work daily. I didn't lose my hair! I attribute all of this to the prayers that were prayed for me.

After the six-week chemo and radiation, I returned to the urologist to see if I needed more treatment. When he looked inside he said it was healing very well and I could stop the treatment. He scheduled a return appointment in four months. At that appointment, he said that it looked very good and there were no signs of cancer. It's been over a year since the operation and I am believing that I am totally healed.

This life and death struggle was fought, first with prayer of the saints, then with the knowledge of man; this knowledge came from God. Proper nutrition, doctors' wisdom, chemical formulas, radiation have always been waiting for man's discovery and proper use. But, the spiritual battle must be fought along with the physical. God is our Father. He is on our side and wants to help when called upon.

How to Combat a Furious Adversary

Satan is having a field day in the blood bought church of Jesus Christ. We in the Body of Christ have allowed him to control our emotions and actions regarding others of the body. He has gotten us to focus on the 20% of Christians who think differently than we do and not on the 80% with whom we can agree. We must understand that Satan is a mathematician – he subtracts and divides!

The Apostle John quoted Jesus in John 10:10 (NIV), *"The thief comes only to steal and kill and destroy; I have come that they may have life, and have it to the full."* This is the huge contrast between Jesus and Satan. Satan is doing everything in his power to steal our lives and soul and Jesus has given us the power to live our lives fully, effectively and victoriously now. Satan tries to steal this joy and fulfilled living from us because he hates us so intensely.

Just this passage of Scripture should be our wakeup call as to the intensity of the battle that we are in. Satan is filled with fury, because he knows that his time is short. Revelation 12:17 (NIV) *"Then the dragon (Satan) was enraged at the woman and went off to make war against the rest of her offspring (us) – those who obey God's commandments and hold to the testimony of Jesus."* That includes you and me, and every Bible believer in every church and denomination that believes Jesus Christ is the only begotten Son of God, born of the virgin Mary, lived a sinless life, was crucified and died on the cross, was buried and on the third day He arose to life and is now seated at the right hand of God interceding on our behalf. You are the target of Satan's wrath!

How do we combat this spiritual power which seems to be so formidable and overpowering? By holding on to and declaring the truth. The church, each one of us, must recognize that we are in a life and death battle and we must stand up and fight!

John 17 is so powerful and important in this struggle and our victory. Please read it three times in a row to help you fully comprehend what we have because of Jesus. Let us look at what Jesus said as recorded in John 17:18, 20 (NIV), *"As You sent me into the world, I have sent them into the world…I pray also for those who will believe in me through their message, that all of them may be one, Father, just as you are in me and I am in you."* We can fight the onslaughts of the enemy with this authority and the Holy Spirit within us just as Jesus did.

Wow! Those two passages are so powerful. If only we can just grasp what Jesus is telling us. Unity is one of the most powerful weapons in our arsenal. This is the exact reason why Satan is in the dividing business; he divided the angels in Heaven, was thrown out, divided Adam and Eve from God, divided Cain and Abel, divides the church today and tries to continually divide marriages, families, pastors, church leaders and on and on! Remember – division – bad; unity – good!

Jesus has paid the price to give you and me the power to overcome the evil supernatural and live in victory today. We must acknowledge that we are in a supernatural war. Ephesians 6:12 (NIV) *"For our struggle is not against flesh and blood, but against the rulers, against the authorities, against the powers of this dark world and against the spiritual forces of evil in heavenly realms."* Jesus didn't deny Satan's authority here on earth as recorded in Matthew. 4:8-10 (NIV), *"Again, the devil took him to a very high mountain and showed him all the kingdoms of the world and their splendor, 'all this I will give to you,' he said, 'if you will bow down and worship me.'"* Jesus was filled with the Holy Spirit after being baptized by John the Baptist and knew the Word of God. These two powerful forces (being filled with the Holy Spirit and knowing the Scriptures) in Jesus overcame Satan and his temptations.

I John 4:4 (NIV), *"You dear children, are from God and have overcome them, because the one who is in you is greater than the one who is in the world."* John. 14:23 (NIV), *"Jesus replied, If anyone loves me, he will obey my teaching. My Father will love him and we will come and make our home with him."* Grasp now the truth that has been given to us by God. The first question that we must answer is do you love Jesus? If the answer is yes, then are you obeying His commands? If that answer is yes, then receive what the

Word says. You are already filled with the Holy Spirit. Then Jesus says, *"My Father will love him and WE will make our home with him."* Now wherever you go, whatever you do, there is a group of four; you, the Father, the Son and the Holy Spirit. Is there anything too hard for this group? Is there anything that you can't overcome? Is there anything too hard for God?

Unity is work. Nothing worth having comes without a price. Jesus paid a price for us because He thought we were worthwhile. As He stepped out of His comfort zone of Heaven, so we must step out of our comfort zone to reach others to help bring unity in our area. We are all "busy" and don't seem to have enough time to get done what we have planned. God is the one who will supply all our needs if we *"seek first His kingdom and His righteousness."* (Matthew 6:33, NIV).

You and I are the ones who control our calendars. If we put our dental appointment on the calendar, we will be there. We need to put on our calendars a time to have breakfast or lunch with some other pastor, ministry leader or someone from another denomination or church so that we can get to know one another better. It's a lot easier to talk against someone you don't know than it is about someone you do. So, let's get to know others better and if the temptation comes to belittle them, we won't submit to that temptation.

Remember, Jesus said in Mark 3:24 (NIV), *"If a kingdom is divided against itself, that kingdom cannot stand."*

We must no longer let our differences divide us. When we do, we are playing in Satan's court. There is nothing more different than men and women, yet God made us that way, then told us to come together and be one! We have done that in marriage, with prayers, even though Paul the Apostle warned us that there would be more trouble in this life for those who marry, I Corinthians 7:28 (AMP), *"Yet those who marry will have physical and earthly troubles, and I would like to spare you that."* Churches are like people with different personalities. We appreciate these personality differences in one another, even though there are clashes at times. As iron sharpens iron, sparks must fly for the edge to become sharper. As we recognize this in our lives, we will come to have more grace and mercy for others and know that we are all growing (being sharpened) to be more like Christ. As you and I grow in love for each other, then the world will come to know Jesus. John. 17:21 (NIV), *"…that all of them may be one, Father, just as you are in me and I in you. May they also be in us so that the world may believe that you have sent me."*

The Importance of Unity

Unity (coming together as one) is so very vital and important for God's people. To fight the spiritual battle – good versus evil – we must all be going in the same direction with the same game plan and purpose. God's will and purpose is that "none should perish" but that all have eternal life both now and forevermore. God has created each of us to accomplish a very special, unique plan while we are here on this earth. Together and doing things God's way, this can be accomplished. This is not about competition, this is about completeness. That is not possible through any one person or any one way. It is not a "one man show," it is not a "one group show," or even a "one nation show". It is each person doing his part, God's way.

You may say to yourself, "How is that possible?" God has purposely made each one of us different. There are times when we are weak and there are times when we are strong. There are things we know and things we don't know. We need each other. God made us this way. Father God, our Heavenly Father, knows all things. It is mandatory that we, God's Children, hear from Him and receive our daily marching orders from The Commander and Chief. God will give you the "what" and "how." When all are listening and obedient, there will be a Divine strategy coming forth. Each battle is different. God will work with a remnant. He always has and this has confounded the wise and learned. God uses those whom the world would consider the most unlikely. Then God receives all the glory.

We must encourage everyone we know to be part of that remnant. Bill and I personally know how exciting it is to be used by the Lord. God wants all His people to enjoy that blessing, not just a select few. God is no respecter of persons and has created each of us to worship Him and to work together in peace, love, unity and one accord. Yes, we are all in a process of being healed, transformed, re-molded and re-made to be more like God and more like Jesus Christ every day.

It's all about souls! It's all about salvations. It's all about spending eternity in Heaven with God – our Creator and Heavenly Father. God knew us before we were born. He knows everything about us.

As Bill and I read Psalm 139 again, the Lord impressed on us that this is the way everlasting He talks about all through the Scriptures. God wants all creation to come back to Him. God made each one of us, but now we must make the decision to acknowledge who He is and the decision to come back to Him. As we read this Psalm in four different versions – King James, Amplified, New American Standard and New International – verse 8 (KJV) stood out, *"If I ascend up into heaven, thou art there; if I make my bed in hell, behold, thou art there."* Then we started thinking about how God made it all and He is everywhere. Satan even had a choice. He was once a beautiful Arch Angel, but he (Satan) tried to overthrow God and take over. God's forces overcame Satan's forces and Satan was thrown out of Heaven. He resides on earth waiting for his time to be cast into the burning lake of fire. His desire is to take as many people with him as possible. That's where we are heading unless we decide to come out of "the kingdom of darkness" (Satan's domain) into the "Kingdom of light" by accepting Jesus Christ as our Lord and Savior.

In Psalm 139:23-24 (NIV) it says, *"Search me, O God, and know my heart: try me, and know my thoughts: And see if there be any wicked way in me, and lead me in the way everlasting."* God wants all of us to invite Jesus Christ to come into our hearts. The whole course of life is made up of trials, tests, challenges, etc. So, we can choose to allow God to remove the wickedness and replace it with His perfect love. God is love!

In the Amplified version, Psalm 139:11-12 (NIV) says, *"If I say, surely the darkness shall cover me and the night shall be (the only) light about me, even the darkness hides nothing from you, but the night shines as the day; the darkness and the light are both alike to you."* In Daniel 2:22 it says, (NKJV), *"He reveals deep and secret things; He knows what is in the darkness, and light dwells with him."*

I (Pam) thought back about a telephone conversation that I once had with a blind woman. I was totally amazed at the spiritual understanding, wisdom and insight this blind lady had about life. She had never "seen" things with her eyes like I had been privileged to see, but the blind lady understood despite living in the darkness. We were both about the same age and we could relate to many of the same things.

Verse 14 of Psalm 139 (NAS) reads, *"I will give thanks to You, for I am fearfully and wonderfully made; wonderful are Your works, and my soul knows it very well."* Bill and I reflected on those times I had been so sick and all the professionals we had gone to who were totally stumped as to what was wrong and how to fix it. God has made our bodies so intricately, and we both thought about how every part needed to work together and help each other so the whole organism could function the way it was created to function. "Thank you, God, for making us so wonderful! You are an Awesome God!"

Psalm 139: 17 – 18 (NAS), *"How precious also are Your thoughts to me, O God! How vast is the sum of them! If I should count them, they would outnumber the sand. When I awake, I am still with You."* We are no accident. It is not just with happenstance that we are here. God has a plan and God has a purpose for each one of us. He loves us and He cares for us and He wants to help us. He's just waiting for us to ask.

Psalm 139:5 - 6 (NIV), *"You hem me in – behind and before; you have laid your hand upon me. Such knowledge is too wonderful for me, too lofty for me to attain."* How comforting it is for us to know God is all around us. We are never alone. He is near to help and to protect us. "Thank You Lord!"

In verse 13 and 14 of Psalm 139 (NIV), *"For you created my inmost being; you knit me together in my mother's womb. I praise you because I am fearfully and wonderfully made; your works are wonderful, I know that full well."* We were designed and fashioned by God. He knows us and He knows all about us. All He is asking from us is that we know Him! God planned our life. Now it's up to us to carry out the plan for which we were created. We are to hate the things God hates and we are to love the things God loves. God loves people, but God hates sin. How can we know and how can we separate the sin from the sinner? Read God's Holy Word, the Bible!

God has set up a rulebook, His Bible, for us to follow. When we don't play by His rules, we suffer the consequences. God is a forgiving God. All we must do is "repent" and say we're sorry and stop doing the wrong and God will forgive us. I John 2:12 (NKJV), *"I write to you, little children, because your sins are forgiven for His name's sake."* God will forgive us, and then we must forgive others. When we are filled with the Father's love, we can do this. Otherwise, it is impossible.

God is continuously wooing us to Himself. We need to give in, give up and surrender to Him. Ask Him to change us and to help us to be more like Jesus. God gave us Jesus, His only begotten Son, to live here on the earth and to be an example to each one of us on how to do things God's way. Jesus would always go to the Father. They were in continuous communication. Jesus said in John 5:19 (NKJV), *"Most assuredly, I say to you, the Son can do nothing by Himself, but what He sees His Father do, for whatever He does, the Son also does in like manner."* How much more do we, His children, need to go to our Heavenly Father?

If you have negative thoughts, feelings or actions that you want to be free from, you must tell God. As an example: "Father, in the name of Jesus Christ of Nazareth, I break the power of (insert name such as fear) in my life, I ask you to replace it with feelings of (insert the opposite-faith and love) in my life. Please set me free from (the negative-fear) and fill me with (the positive-faith and love)."

God has brought many different people into our lives from many different walks of life and many different nations. We have learned from and grown spiritually through these interactions and exchanges of ideas and beliefs. America has always been the "big brother" to other nations and now God needs America to come back to Him and stand up and fight the good fight, the spiritual fight, to get back that which has been lost. The moral backbone of this society needs to reflect God's values as He has set forth in His Holy Word, the Bible. We declare that we are truly *"One Nation Under God!"*

THE BATTLE BELONGS TO THE LORD

The Lord has given us victory already! All of our hurts, pain, sorrow, illness, concerns, etc., were nailed to the cross with Jesus over 2000 years ago. In Isaiah 53:4-5 (NIV) we read, *"Surely he took up our infirmities and carried our sorrows, yet we considered him stricken by God, smitten by him, and afflicted. But he was pierced for our transgressions, he was crushed for our iniquities; the punishment that brought us peace was upon him, and by his wounds we are healed."*

And in I Peter 2:24 (NIV), *"He himself bore our sins in his body on the tree, so that we might die to sins and live for righteousness: by his wounds you have been healed."* This is so powerful that the Apostle Peter restates what God spoke through Isaiah concerning the victory and peace that God's children have now due to what Jesus did for us at Calvary.

John 14:27 (AMP), *"Peace I leave with you; My (own) peace I now give and bequeath to you. Not as the world gives do I give to you. Do not let your hearts be troubled, neither let them be afraid."* Part of what Jesus did on the cross was to secure for each one of His followers a life of peace. The wounds that He bore have brought us healing for all of our problems and a peace that surpasses all understanding as we live in this world, this battleground, for our minds, bodies and souls.

II Corinthians 6:79 (NIV) tells us, "... *with weapons of righteousness in the right hand and the left...*" We are now able to fight the good fight and be victorious in all areas of our lives. Being righteous means doing things the right way, God's way.

We must always remember, even though we are in a fight, God gives us the weapons for victory. II Corinthians 10:3-5 (NIV) tells us, "*The weapons we fight with are not the weapons of the world. On the contrary, they have divine power to demolish strongholds. We demolish arguments and every pretention that sets itself up against the knowledge of God, and we take captive every thought.*"

God makes it very clear in the Bible that we have available to us all that is needed to stand up and fight and be victorious!

The object of any war is to defeat the enemy. An enemy in the conventional sense is a person or group of people, driven by greed, power and ego, who will do anything to get what you have. Many wars are fought over ideology or religion. This means that their goal is to change our beliefs to suit theirs. They want to rid us of the freedom that we have to believe and to live a certain way. The enemy must overcome our opposition by deceit or overt action to destroy his opposing force through death, wounding, capturing and conquering. This is exactly what the apostle John tells us in John 10:10 (NIV), *"The thief comes only to steal, kill and destroy; I have come that they may have life, and have it to the full."* Jesus is telling us of the spiritual battle that is going on between Him and Satan for us. Satan wants to steal from us all that Jesus gave His life for in providing us with a life of peace. Satan's goal is to destroy and kill us to plunder God's kingdom and populate his.

WE ARE OUR OWN WORST ENEMY!

This is war. We must stand up and fight and say no to every deceit of the enemy to defeat us and take us captive. One of the largest problems in the church today is un-forgiveness. We want forgiveness but, we are unwilling to forgive someone who, we feel, has wronged us in some way. This is a tremendous open door for Satan to come in and wreak havoc in our lives. Most of us are chained to someone (or many) because of what they have done or said to us that has hurt us in some way. We are unwilling to forgive because they have done something to hurt our feelings. Satan helps us with our justification of withholding our forgiveness. Justification is the great deceit of Satan to help in our downfall. Now we are living in disobedience to our Lord which aids Satan with his activities in our life and cuts off the peace that Jesus has provided for us.

It is interesting that when Jesus' disciples asked him to teach them how to pray, He taught them what we call the Lord's Prayer as found in Matthew 6:9-13 (AMP), *"Pray, therefore like this: Our Father who is in heaven, hallowed (kept holy) be Your name. Your kingdom come, Your will be done on earth as it is in heaven. Give us this day our daily bread. And forgive us our debts, as we also have forgiven (left, remitted, and let go of the debts, and have given up resentment against) our debtors. And lead (bring) us not into temptation, but deliver us from the evil one, for Yours is the kingdom and the power and the glory forever. Amen."*

After the prayer, Jesus expounds on one portion of the prayer dealing with forgiveness. He must have known what a problem this would be for his disciples, to forgive those who have hurt them in some way. Matthew 6:14-15 (NIV), *"For if you forgive men when they sin against you, your heavenly Father will also forgive you. But, if you do not forgive men their sins, your Father will not forgive your sins."* The door of unforgiveness of others must be closed to stop the attack of the enemy in this area of our lives and for us to be able to be partakers of the divine peace given through the cross.

Before your salvation, while you were in unforgiveness, the only way you could fight a spiritual battle was in the natural. Satan will run circles around us if we try to fight in the natural. Jesus has given to us the Holy Spirit so that our battles can be fought in the spiritual with God's power to defeat the enemy. The following verse is so powerful and we must remember it and put it into use as often as is necessary (daily if need be), I John 4:4 (NAS), *"You, dear children, are from God and have overcome them, because the one who is in you is greater than the one who is in the world."* We are God's dear children. He loves you and me so much that He allowed His Son to die for our sins and bring reconciliation between us and God! We are from God and we have overcome them (Satan and his demonic forces) because of God's Spirit that resides in us. The Spirit in us does spiritual battle with the evil supernatural to bring us the victory. Ephesians 6:12 (NIV), *"For our struggle is not against flesh and blood, but against the rulers, against the authorities, against the powers of this dark world and against the spiritual forces of evil in the heavenly realms."* We cannot gain victory by our own intellect, training, cunning ways, scheming or any other natural insights that we might have. Satan can only be defeated in the spiritual realm by allowing the battle to belong to the Lord's.

Our God is the God of the present. Hebrews 13:8 (NIV) says, *"Jesus Christ is the same yesterday and today and forever."* And in I Peter 2:24 (AMP), *"...by His (Jesus) wounds you have been healed."* The wording "have been healed" makes this statement present tense. Yet, we Christians continue to walk around in defeat with a bad case of "woe is me"! Our own actions open doors for the evil supernatural to come in and hinder our walk of victory. Again, let us state that one of the most prevalent problems in the church today is the unforgiveness we hold against another person. This is so important for us to understand.

We want our sins and transgressions forgiven by God, but if someone says something that we don't like or take offense to, we go into retaliation mode. When you make that decision to be offended and withhold forgiveness, you have opened the door for demonic influence in your life. The demonic forces help you to think of that other person very negatively. You start feeling justified for your feeling which puts a deeper chasm between you and them. Your stomach begins to churn and you avoid them and sit on the opposite side of the church. This feeling of justification for your feelings and hurt is Satan's way of keeping you in bondage where you will not walk in victory and peace.

This is as plain as it gets. Our actions will either open the doors for God to come in and work in our lives or our actions will close the doors to God and open them to the evil supernatural. Let's grow up and grow beyond this age-old tactic of Satan's. Our war is not against flesh and blood, but if Satan can keep us warring in the natural, he is off the hook. Think now, of everyone who has hurt you in any way. Take a moment to talk with God and tell Him about the person and how they offended you. Tell Him how you feel about them; your anger, hurt, frustration, etc.

Then say, "God, I choose to forgive (say the person's name) for (the offense) and not hold that against them anymore. Please forgive me for withholding my forgiveness. Father, now that I have spoken forgiveness to (say the name), would You please heal the hurt that they caused me?" You are now releasing to God this situation and giving God the opportunity to come in and heal your wounds and to take proper action upon the one who has hurt you. Until you have completed this action, God's hands are off of you and the other person.

"Do not conform any longer to the pattern of this world, but be transformed by the renewing of your mind," Romans 12:2 (NIV). By saying the prayer above, you have begun the process of renewing your mind. If Satan tries to bring back the old thoughts, just say, "I praise the Lord; I am set free and totally forgiven." Read the Bible daily to renew and refresh your mind. And remember, I John 4:4 (NIV), *"You, dear children, are from God and have overcome them, because the one who is in you, is greater than the one who is in the world."*

The Spirit Man

When we are in the heat of the battle, yes, even when you don't know which end is up, the spirit man within you needs to "stand up and fight" for you. The spirit within you needs to rise and take authority over the flesh. You may say, "I feel so weak I can't seem to fight. Not only can I not seem to fight, I can't seem to think clearly". The things that I had always done and seemed to come so naturally like prayer, reading the Bible, listening to God, were virtually impossible for me. I knew this was part of my weaponry against the evil supernatural forces that were bombarding my mind, but I couldn't seem to overcome. Many, many times I would read the Bible but had no comprehension of what it was saying.

I (Pam) couldn't remember a word of what I had read. I couldn't think of how to pray, even if something or someone would come to my mind. Through the reading of the Bible, the spirit man within was still being refreshed and renewed for future battles. Looking back now, I feel God used some of those "stored up prayers" I had prayed in times past. Revelation 5:8 says (NIV), *"Each one had a harp and they were holding bowls full of incense which are the prayers of the saints."*

On October 2, 2004, Bill and I put out a spiritual SOS to our entire e-mail list as we knew we needed the unified Body of Christ to stand with us in this spiritual battle. We knew that this was a spiritual attack from the evil supernatural and needed spiritual reinforcements to overcome.

It was so encouraging for us to receive e-mails, phone calls and letters from prayer partners. Many times, as we traveled for speaking engagements people would come up to us and say that they had been praying for us. Many were people that we didn't even know! That was so uplifting to us. We would thank them and I would tell them how much their prayers had helped in clearing my mind. It was truly the prayers of the saints that sustained us. And we continue to believe that I will be totally healed with the manifestation of a peaceful, restful night's sleep without having to take medication.

Prayers are a fragrant aroma to God! He loves to hear from us and He loves to speak to us. He created us to worship Him. Psalms 145:18 (NIV) says, *"The Lord is near to all who call on him in truth."*

One night I (Pam) had a dream about a jogger (I now believe he was an angel) who was a man, but very nondescript as to nationality. He passed me and turned his head and said, "Isaiah 48:8-18." I awoke and thought that I had experienced things like this before, so I didn't want to lose this. I reached for a pen and paper and wrote down the Scripture. It just kept going over in my mind. I finally fell back to sleep and the next morning, when I awoke; I picked up my Bible to see what the passage said.

"You have neither heard nor understood; from of old your ear has not been open. Well do I know how treacherous you are; you were called a rebel from birth. 9 For my own name's sake I delay my wrath; for the sake of my praise I hold it back from you, so as not to cut you off. 10 See, I have refined you, though not as silver; I have tested you in the furnace of affliction. 11 For my own sake, I do this. How can I let myself be defamed? I will not yield my glory to another. 12 Listen to me, O Jacob, Israel, whom I have called; I am he; I am the first and the last. 13 My own hand laid the foundations of the earth, and my right hand laid out the heavens; when I summon them, they all stand up together. 14 Come together, all of you, and listen: Which of the idols has foretold these things? The Lord's chosen ally will carry out his purpose against Babylon, his arm will be against the Babylonians; 15 I, even I, have spoken; yes, I have called him. I will bring him, and he will succeed in his mission. 16 Come near me and listen to this: From the first announcement I have not spoken in secret; at the time it happens, I am there. And now the Sovereign Lord has sent me, with his spirit. 17 This is what the Lord says – your Redeemer, the Holy One of Israel: "I am the Lord your God, who teaches you what is best for you, who directs you in the way you should go. 18 If only you had paid attention to my commands, your peace

would have been like a river, your righteousness like the waves of the sea" (Isaiah 48:8-18, NIV).

After reading this passage the Lord showed me that it is He who allows problems in our lives to help in our growth and changes us to be more like Him to better equip us for the call that He has on our life. In other words, God sent problems to try to make the Israelites change when they got off course and come back to His will and desires for them. He allows problems in our lives to get our attention and turn us back to Him or to help us grow to become all that He wants us to be. Only He knows how to train us for His work here. Thank you, Lord, for chastising and guiding us out of Your love for us!

GOD'S ARMY

Are you in God's Army? This is a question we must all ask ourselves. When we accept Jesus, we join His Army. Our boot camp should be discipleship training. New recruits are unprepared. Matthew 13:3-8 (NKJ) parable of the seed.

> *"Behold, a sower went out to sow. And as he sowed, some seed fell by the wayside; and the birds came and devoured them. Some fell on stony places, where they did not have much earth; they immediately sprang up because they had no depth of earth. But when the sun was up they were scorched, and because they had no root they withered away. And some fell among thorns, and the thorns sprang up and choked them. But others fell on good ground and yielded a crop: some a hundredfold, some sixty, some thirty."*

Satan wants to snatch the Word from us because he knows that it will produce a crop of 30-60-100-fold. We're either "in" or we're not. We're on God's side or we're not.

God promises us in His Word, that He will fight our fight, however, He does require things from us first.

As He points out so clearly in Ephesians 6:10, 13-18 (NKJ),

> *"My brethren, be strong in the Lord and in the power of His might…Therefore take up the whole armor of God, that you may be able to withstand in the evil day; and having done all, to stand. Stand therefore, having girded your waist with truth, having put on the breastplate of righteousness, and having shod your feet with the preparation of the gospel of peace; above all, taking the shield of faith with which you will be able to quench all the fiery darts of the wicked one. And take the helmet of salvation, and the sword of the Spirit, which is the word of God; Praying always with all prayer and supplication in the Spirit, being watchful to this all perseverance and supplication for all the saints…"*

Just as in the physical military, we, also, can be POW'S (prisoners of war). We can be so *"bound up,"* *"chained up,"* or *"rendered useless"* by our past, that we're unable to be effective for the Lord. Deliverance ministry "sets the captives free!"

We can also go AWOL (absent without leave). We just want to enjoy the blessings the Christian life offers, but when it comes to any sufferings we're "out of there." We know many Christians who don't even believe that

Satan exists! They don't understand that we are physically living out a spiritual war.

We had a friend tell us she would pray for us as we went into the city of San Francisco, CA to go to a prayer meeting on Halloween night. In her eyes, we could tell that she certainly couldn't go along with our way of thinking. She really couldn't believe that going into the city to pray with approximately 8,000 other Christians would do much good. She felt that individual prayers prayed anywhere would be just as good. But, the unity of believers praying together in one accord is spiritually very powerful! Remember, "they were all in one accord, praying together" and the Holy Spirit fell on them. Prayer and unity in the Body of Christ is supernaturally powerful.

It's hard for us to believe today that Christians think witchcraft, Satanism and other forms of evil are non-existent. But up until the mid-eighties when I was so sick with an immune system illness, Bill and I were unaware of the extent of the evil supernatural. God opened our eyes and we started looking at the Bible, life and happenings in a totally different way.

We are still going through many challenges in our lives now, where God is teaching us new things. This is a continuing process for us all until we are called "home". He is still helping us to understand that we need to stand on His promises in the Bible regardless of what it looks like or feels like. Some of the "curses" we felt had been put on us by the evil supernatural, are curses we had spoken on ourselves. The words that we speak are powerful and can be uplifting or destructive. Ephesians 4:29 says, *"Do not let any unwholesome talk come out of your mouths, but only what is helpful for building others up…"* We must always remember that when Jesus spoke, spiritual things happened; seas subsided, winds died down, people were healed or raised from the dead. Then He said, *"As the Father has sent Me, I am sending you."* The Holy Spirit that resided in Jesus is the same Holy Spirit in us. So, when we speak, spiritual things happen. That is why it is so important to watch the way we speak.

As God opens your eyes, as He opened ours, be quick to confess sin, repent and break the power of those angry words spoken. As a friend of ours said: "Don't be discouraged by what you see and hear, but be encouraged by what you know and believe." We believe the Lord is having us go directly to His Word and stand on His truth, His promises and His Word in all areas of our lives.

God's Army is made up of many branches, just as the physical armed forces are made up of; the Army, Navy, Air Force, Marines and Coast Guard. There are the regular troops, the leaders, the Green Berets, the Delta Force, the Navy Seals, etc. We all have a position and it's only in that position where God's anointing will flow. Why do we try to do what someone else has been called to do? Why are we so competitive, jealous and envious regarding what God has anointed someone else to do? We all need to do our job, stay in our position and use the gifts and talents God has given to us. We must pray to be filled with God's love for each other and we must work together in peace and unity to take our cities back for Jesus Christ and the United States of America...one nation under God (the Creator of this universe). God is love!

THE BRIDE

The Church is like the immune system, fighting off infection, impurities and disease. The evil forces of darkness (Satan and his kingdom) are out to kill, steal and destroy. Destruction can only come when the resistance is low. James 4:7-8 (NKJV), *"Therefore submit to God. Resist the devil and he will flee from you. Draw near to God and He will draw near to you."*

God is working individually and corporately on each of us so that "His church, His Bride" the Body of Christ will be strong. God tells us that temptation will be strong and try to overcome us, but He will give us a way out. We must live a pure and holy life. We must be strong in the Lord and well-grounded in His Word. Jesus resisted Satan (Matthew 4:1-11) by responding "It is written." Even when Satan twisted the Word of God, Jesus spoke it exactly as it is written in the Scriptures. Satan attacks in the physical realm; he attacks our mind and truth; think of Eve in the garden when the serpent said, (Genesis 3:4. NIV), *"You will not surely die, the serpent said to the woman. For God knows that when you eat of it your eyes will be opened, and you will be like God, knowing good and evil."* In these end times in which we are living, it is the written Word that will defeat the forces of darkness. We must know the Word, speak the Word and stand on the promises in FAITH! Faith is what pleases God, *"without faith it is impossible to please and be satisfactory to*

Him" (Hebrews 11:6, AMP). Faith comes by hearing and hearing by the Word of God.

How is your "Word" weaponry? John 14 is one of the most powerful chapters in the Bible! Verse twenty-three demonstrates our point if we can only grasp the truth that Jesus is telling us, (NIV), *"If anyone loves Me, he will obey My teaching. My Father will love him, and we will come and make our home with him."* If we are filled with the Holy Spirit and doing the will of Jesus, the Word tells us that wherever we go there will be four; you, the Holy Spirit, Jesus and Father God! With this group, what can be too difficult for you?

"Let us rejoice and shout for joy (exulting and triumphant)! Let us celebrate and ascribe to Him glory and honor, for the marriage of the Lamb (at last) has come, and His bride has prepared herself" (Revelation 19:7, AMP). We are the Bride of Christ and as this Scripture tells us, we must prepare ourselves. The first way of preparation is to know His Word and then do it. Could we be holding up His second coming because we are not prepared?

Memorization hasn't come easy to us. Some people just read the Word and can remember everything they have read. We must know and understand how much power there is in prayer, so let's pray right now for ourselves to be able to readily speak forth the accurate Word of God, as we need it to fight off the enemy. "We ask You, God, to help us remember Your Word as we read it and to be able to access it as we need it. Help us to be encouraged by Your Word, God. To believe what You say to be the truth. Help us to know immediately when Your Word is quoted incorrectly. Help us fight this good fight of faith and gain victory as our strength comes from You. In Jesus' name, we pray."

The Lord is good. His mercy is everlasting, and His truth endures to all generations. We must be a carrier of this truth. We must be a believer, and we must step out in faith as we claim the victory. We are new creatures in Christ, ready to give an account of the hope which lies within us. We are victorious and we are winners. Remember, we are men and women of faith!

Ask God to show you His end time strategy. Ask Him for revelation insight and understanding and then ask Him how to apply it. He will show you! All He wants us to do is ask. He is ready, willing and more than able to answer. The hope lies within each one of us. We are to always be ready to share this with whomever the Lord brings into our lives.

The following is from "The Gospel Soul Winning Script" from *Revival Ministries International*, PO Box 292888, Tampa, FL 33687, (813) 971-9999.

> "Has anyone ever told you that God loves you and that He has a wonderful plan for your life? I have a quick, but important question to ask you. If you were to die this very second, do you know for sure, beyond

a shadow of a doubt, that you would go to Heaven? If yes, great, but why would you say that? If you responded with anything but 'I have Jesus in my heart' or something like that; proceed with script. Or if you answer 'no' or 'I hope so' proceed with script.

Let me quickly share with you what the Holy Bible reads. It reads 'for all have sinned and come short of the glory of God' and 'for the wages of sin is death, but the gift of God is eternal life through Jesus Christ our Lord'. The Bible also reads, 'For whosoever shall call upon the name of the Lord shall be saved'. And you're a 'whosoever', right? Of course, you are; all of us are.

I'm going to say a quick prayer for you. "Lord bless (insert your name) and his/her family with long and healthy lives. Jesus, make Yourself real to him/her and do a quick work in him/her heart. If (insert name) has not received Jesus Christ as his/her Lord and Savior, I pray he/she will do so now.

(Fill in name), if you would like to receive the gift that God has for you today, say this after me with your heart and lips out loud. 'Dear Lord Jesus, come into my heart. Forgive me of my sin. Wash me and cleanse me. Set me free. Jesus, thank You that You died for me. I believe that You are risen from the dead and that You're coming back again for me. Fill me with the Holy Spirit. Give me a passion for the lost, a hunger for the things of God and a holy boldness to preach the gospel of Jesus Christ. I'm saved, I'm born again, I'm forgiven and I'm on my way to Heaven because I have Jesus in my heart.

As a minister of the gospel of Jesus Christ, I tell you today that all your sins are forgiven. Always remember to run to God and not from Him because He loves you and has a great plan for your life.

Encourage them to go and find a Bible believing church and begin attending. They need to have fellowship with other believers, be baptized by immersion in water, to be discipled and to read their Bible and pray daily."

Praying for Our Nation

Our nation was founded on the principles of God. Our founding fathers knew the importance of prayer and Scripture. Today each one of us needs to seek the counsel of the Lord to see what our part is in bringing this nation back to God. In and of ourselves we are nothing, but with Him, and the Holy Spirit's help, all things are possible. Our Father, God, has sent His Son, Jesus Christ, to be our Lord and Savior, the ultimate sacrifice. Jesus is our model and example. He was and is a man of prayer. He only did what the Father told Him to do and said what the Holy Father told Him to say. How much more do we, His children, need to seek the wise council of God and be obedient to what He asks of us.

Jesus is seated at the right hand of God interceding for you and me. This is how important prayer is and hearing the voice of God. We don't have any time to waste. God needs us to be His spokespeople here on earth to others around us and to be interceding on behalf of our nation.

> *"If My people who are called by My name, will humble themselves and pray and seek My face and turn from their wicked ways, then will I hear from heaven and will forgive their sin and will heal their land"* (II Chronicles 7:14, NIV).

This is God's promise to us if we do our part. What is our part? To repent, pray and listen to God. We CAN make a difference. If we say we are Christians, we must be men and women of prayer as Jesus was. We must emulate the life of Jesus when He was here on earth for His will was and is that none should perish, but that all should have eternal life.

We need to have personal prayer time. As a couple, we need to pray together. As a family, we need to pray together. This is a part of raising our children in the way they should go. They need to see you in prayer alone, in prayer with your spouse and in prayer as a family. Then there should be small group prayer and prayer with your church. Partake in city prayer gatherings, prayerwalk your neighborhood and intercede for others. Some targets of your intercession should be your family, church, pastors, schools, neighborhoods, those in authority, leaders, government (local, state and national), media and world situations to name a few.

This is how we bring America back to God; one step at a time, one prayer at a time. Persevere, be steadfast and be diligent. Keep pounding the wall! It will come down in Jesus' name. God will honor your time and effort spent with Him. James 1:2-4 (NIV), *"Consider it pure joy, my brothers, whenever you face trials of many kinds, because you know that the testing of your faith develops perseverance. Perseverance must finish its work so that you may be mature and complete, not lacking anything."*

Thank God for everything. He can take all things and work them together for good. It's during the hard times that God gives us an opportunity to grow and become more like Jesus. It's these trials that develop us more into what God desires us to be. We must be different than the world in the way we look, dress and act. Seduction is not God's way. His desires for us are purity, peace (in all circumstances), love and unity; united we stand, divided we fall.

Each one of us in this great nation, the United States of America, must work together to once again unify this nation and help other nations to be one nation under God. God has given us His rule book, the Bible, to be our source of truth in guiding our lives and helping others with theirs. This book holds the promises we can stand on and move forward in victory. It assures us that our prayers will be heard as we pray according to His will. His will is found on the pages of His Scriptures. Matthew 6:33 (NIV), *"But seek first His kingdom and His righteousness…"*

So, let's wake up America while there is still time. We can make a difference! Let's start today and see what God will do with our obedience.

"We thank You, God, for the city that we live in. We thank you, God, for the state we live in. We thank

You, God, for our great nation. May You give guidance and wisdom to every governmental official so that we may live in peace and have Your name lifted high always. We pray these things in the mighty, wonderful and powerful name of the Lord, Jesus Christ, our Lord and Savior. Amen."

A Gift of The Spirit

The Holy Spirit has been authorized to bestow different gifts to different people in the Body of Christ. These gifts are meant to work together to help in building up the entire body together and to bring glory to our Father. Below is a rendering of just one of the gifts available. As can be seen, not all are given the same gifts, but all gifts are given to individuals so that the body may work in unison in bringing others into His kingdom and glory to the Giver.

> Jesus says, *"And these signs will follow those who believe: In My name, they will cast out demons; they will speak with new tongues..."* (Mark 16:17, NKJV).
>
> *"And when Paul had laid hands on them, the Holy Spirit came upon them, and they spoke with tongues and prophesied"* (Acts 19:6, NKJV).
>
> *"There are diversities of gifts, but the same Spirit. There are differences of ministries, but the same Lord. And there are diversities of activities, but it is the same God who works all in all. But the manifestation of the Spirit is given to each one for the profit of all: for to one is given the word of wisdom through the Spirit, to another the word of knowledge through the same Spirit,*

to another faith by the same Spirit, to another the gifts of healings by the same Spirit, to another the working of miracles, to another prophecy, to another discerning of spirits to another different kinds of tongues, to another the interpretation of tongues. But one and the same Spirit works all these things, distributing to each one individually as He wills" (I Corinthians 12:4-11, NKJV).

"Do all have gifts of healings? Do all speak with tongues? Do all interpret? But earnestly desire the best gifts" (I Corinthians 12:30-31, NKJV).

"He who speaks in a tongue edifies himself, but he who prophesies edifies the church. I wish you all spoke with tongues, but even more that you prophesied; for he who prophesies is greater than he who speaks with tongues, unless indeed he interprets, that the church may receive edification" (I Corinthians 14:4-5, NKJV).

"I thank my God I speak with tongues more than you all…" (I Corinthians 14:18, NKJV).

"But you, beloved, building yourselves up on your most holy faith, praying in the Holy Spirit" (Jude 20, NKJV).

Pam and I started our Christian walk in a church that did not believe in speaking in tongues. It was never talked about nor taught. The Scripture, I Corinthians 13:10 (NKJV), *"But when that which is perfect has come, then that which is in part will be done away,"* was used to explain that speaking in tongues was no longer valid for today. Many people feel that this passage refers to the canon of the Scriptures being completed around the end of the first century. But, the Scripture instructs us to welcome the Holy Spirit's gifts and ministries into our lives. Most biblical scholars and Bible commentaries feel that this Scripture refers to the final coming of our Lord, Jesus Christ. He is the perfect one and all things will be made perfect at His coming.

Pam became very sick in the mid 1980's and the doctors could not diagnose what it was nor a treatment for her. She had to resign from her very demanding and high profile job because she had no energy and couldn't concentrate on her work. We became very desperate for answers and a solution to this predicament.

A friend told us of a healing conference in San Francisco that she was attending and would we like to go? I didn't have faith for this kind of teaching, but I told Pam that she could go if she wanted. Pam did go with her friend the next day. When she came home I started in with questions as to what they were teaching and what she had learned. She told me that it seemed very good with much Scripture and teaching that seemed "right on." She said that I would have to come and find out for myself as she couldn't remember all that was taught.

The next day was Saturday and the last day of the conference, so I (Bill) said that I would go with them. They taught from Scripture right out of the Bible, but much of the Scripture I had classified being done away with in the first century. They were using it as though these Scriptures pertained to today. At the end of the day they had people who needed healing to come forward and they would pray for them as the rest of us observed and learned from the experience.

One of the things stated was that it was not necessary to pray in tongues, but if you had been given that gift, it seemed to be more powerful. This was my first experience with praying in tongues. Pam received prayer and said that she felt better, but was not healed. I didn't think much more about the tongues aspect, but I feel the Lord placed a seed of desire in me that day.

A few weeks later, we heard of another healing conference taking place at a Chinese Christian Center close to us. Pam wanted to attend that as they were having English speaking teachers and it was translated into Chinese. I (Bill) was unable to attend as I was working at the time, so Pam went alone. Each day she would receive prayer from one of the Chinese pastors who prayed in Chinese and tongues. We knew this because the pastor told Pam that she was praying both ways as the Spirit led her. Every day Pam would come home with a little more strength and energy.

After the conference, she was invited back at any time. Pam started going to this center, Agape Renewal Center, in Belmont, CA, because she felt such peace and could read her Bible and receive prayer. Soon I started going and became acquainted with the Pastor, Dr. Ernest Chan. We would all go together to different conferences and became very good friends. When Pastor Chan felt that it was time had come to start a Chinese church at Agape, he asked us if we would teach the children, who spoke English. We, of course felt honored and accepted. We worked many years with Pastor Chan and our ministry, Pray U.S.A. was birthed out of Agape.

During this time, he hosted many top Christian speakers from across the United States and some from China. We were so blessed to be able to sit in the teaching of these great men and women of God. Many of them spoke of receiving the gift of tongues and many of them prayed for us to receive this gift. Our desire was to receive this gift, but it never took place. This, of course, was disappointing.

Pam was sick approximately seven years and during that time, we lost our home, cars, jobs and were deep in debt. During a time when there seemed to be no hope, we prayed together for God to take her home. No doctor had an answer, no medicine helped, she would cough continuously all night, why remain here? But, this wasn't God's plan. When she started getting better I was so happy and praised and thanked God for her healing.

But, just saying, "thank you" seemed so inadequate to me it didn't really express what my true inner joy and happiness was.

It was at this point that as I was worshipping God that the Holy Spirit conferred upon me my desired gift of speaking in tongues. As I began speaking in my new language, I could feel a release of gratitude within me to Father for His healing of Pam. Soon after, Pam also received her gift of tongues. There was nothing that we did to earn what we received. It was a gift.

VICTORY IN JESUS

He has won the victory for us!

Because of His victory, we can have peace on the inside regardless of what is going on around us. We can't change the situations or the circumstances, but we can change our attitude towards them. This is when we go to God in prayer and say, "Lord, help me to be more Christ-like. Show me what Jesus would do, what He would say and how He would respond. Lord, I do want to change and not react so much out of my flesh, but more out of my spirit. Help my spirit to rise and take authority over my flesh and help me to learn what it is that You want me to learn from this situation. I desire to die to myself and my selfishness and to be more of a servant, like You, Jesus. Thank You, Lord!

> *"For God so greatly loved and dearly prized the world that He [even] gave up His only begotten (unique) Son, so that whoever believes in (trusts in, clings to, relies on) Him shall not perish (come to destruction, be lost) but have eternal (everlasting) life"* (John 3:16, AMP).

The love that we feel here on earth for our families; wives, husbands, children, etc., is so fabulous and it makes us feel so good and accepted. God's love for us is so much more and unchanging. There are no words available to explain how deeply He loves us. He has tried to show us by allowing His Son to come and live a victorious life here and then die for us on the cross, taking our sins with Him and then defeating the grave by being resurrected on the third day. The victory He won on the cross and in the grave, is also the victory He has given us.

> *"For whatever is born of God is victorious over the world; and this is the victory that conquers the world, even our faith. Who is it that is victorious over [that conquers] the world but he who believes that Jesus is the Son of God [who adheres to, trusts in, and relies on that fact]?"* (I John 5:4-5, AMP)

As we accept Jesus as our Lord and Savior, ask Him to come and live in our hearts, we also receive this victory that conquers the world. We still must fight the daily battles, but we do it with the knowledge that the victory is already won and we are the winners because we belong to Jesus.

> *"Yet amid all these things we are more than conquerors and gain a surpassing victory through Him Who loved us"* (Romans 8:37, AMP).

Each struggle, trial, temptation, He allows for us to be able to grow into the person He wants us to be. He knows what He has created in us and He knows what

He would like us to accomplish. He will never give us more than we can handle, but will always make a way to overcome any obstacle. (I Cor. 9:22 para.) Through these struggles, we gain a *"surpassing victory through Him who loves us."*

> *"I have told you these things, so that in Me you may have [perfect] peace and confidence. In the world, you have tribulation and trials and distress and frustration; but be of good cheer [take courage; be confident, certain, undaunted]! For I have overcome the world. [I have deprived it of power to harm you and have conquered it for you.]"* (John 16:33, AMP)

Because of what the creator of the universe has already done for us, we are able to have perfect peace. Our heartaches, frustrations and failures are only temporary setbacks that help us gain patience and perseverance. Jesus has overcome the world and because He lives in us, we also, have already overcome the world.

> *"May grace (God's unmerited favor) and spiritual peace [which means peace with God and harmony, unity, and undisturbedness] be yours from God our Father and from the Lord Jesus Christ"* (Ephesians 1:2, AMP).

Peace, joy, happiness, contentment, etc., are ours now because we know that *"all things work together for good to those who love God..."* (Romans 8:28, NIV). This is why and how we can live a life of peace now.

> *"And to keep me from being puffed up and too much elated by the exceeding greatness (preeminence) of these revelations, there was given me a thorn (a splinter) in the flesh, a messenger of Satan, to rack and buffet and harass me, to keep me from being excessively exalted. (Job2:6) Three time I called upon the Lord and besought (Him) about this and begged that it might depart from me. But He said to me, My grace (My favor and loving kindness and mercy) is enough for you (sufficient against any danger and enables you to bear the trouble manfully); for My strength and power are made perfect (fulfilled and completed) and show themselves most effective in (your) weakness. Therefore, I will all the more gladly glory in my weakness and infirmities, that the strength and power of Christ (the Messiah) may rest (yes, may pitch a tent and dwell) upon me"* (II Corinthians 1:11-12, AMP).

Today, as this book is being finished, I (Pam) am still fighting the good fight against my infirmities. I continue to need medication for sleep. I've recently been diagnosed with rheumatoid arthritis and have pain throughout my body. But, much improvement has been made, and Bill and I continue to believe for a total healing. God is our healer and He can heal instantly, over time or not at all as was the case with the Apostle Paul. Remember that our trials and tribulations are to help equip us so that we may be better able to help others. With a test comes our testimony.

I serve as a volunteer on the Christian Television Network's prayer line. Due to my trials, I can relate by experience to so many callers and minister much more effectively to others struggling with infirmities and tough life issues. I also use the Gospel Soul Winning Script (mentioned earlier) to lead many to Christ.

> *Strengthened with all might, according to His glorious power, for all patience and longsuffering with joy; giving thanks to the Father who has qualified us to be partakers of the inheritance of the saints in the light. He has delivered us from the power of darkness and conveyed us into the kingdom of the Son of His love, in whom we have redemption through His blood, the forgiveness of sins"* (Colossians 1:11-14, NKJV).

Having joy amid a problem doesn't seem to be a natural human quality. Yet, the Apostle Paul said that he learned to be content in all circumstances, so this is a quality that we all may learn. Intellectually, we know that the Bible says that it is in rough times that we are given a chance to grow. So, go by faith and ask God to help you have joy during a problem, knowing that He has allowed the problem for your growth. This is how we know He loves us; His desire for us to grow.

> *"I have fought the good fight, I have kept the faith. Now there is in store for me the crown of righteousness, which the Lord, the righteous Judge, will award to me on that day – and not only me, but also to all who have longed for His appearing"* (II Timothy 4:7-8, NIV).

Now our reward awaits. He will crown us with righteousness along with all the other saints. We have victory in Jesus. Thank you, Lord!

> *"BELOVED, I PRAY THAT YOU MAY PROSPER IN ALL THINGS AND BE IN HEALTH, JUST AS YOUR SOUL PROSPERS"* (III John 2, NKJV).

The Authors

Bill and Pam Malone
P. O. Box 22066
St. Petersburg, FL 33742
727-524-7729
prayusasf@aol.com

www.ingramcontent.com/pod-product-compliance
Lightning Source LLC
Chambersburg PA
CBHW070542300426
44113CB00011B/1765